Japanese Kites

Edel Wignell

CELEBRATION PRESS

Pearson Learning Group

Map of the World

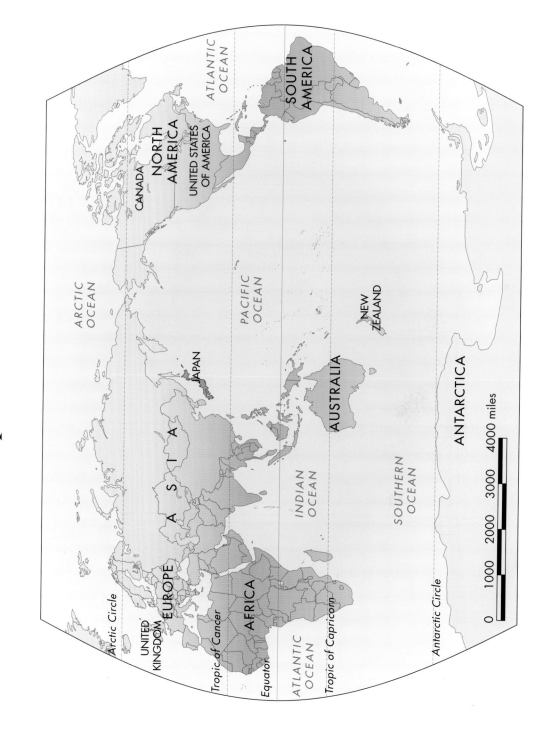

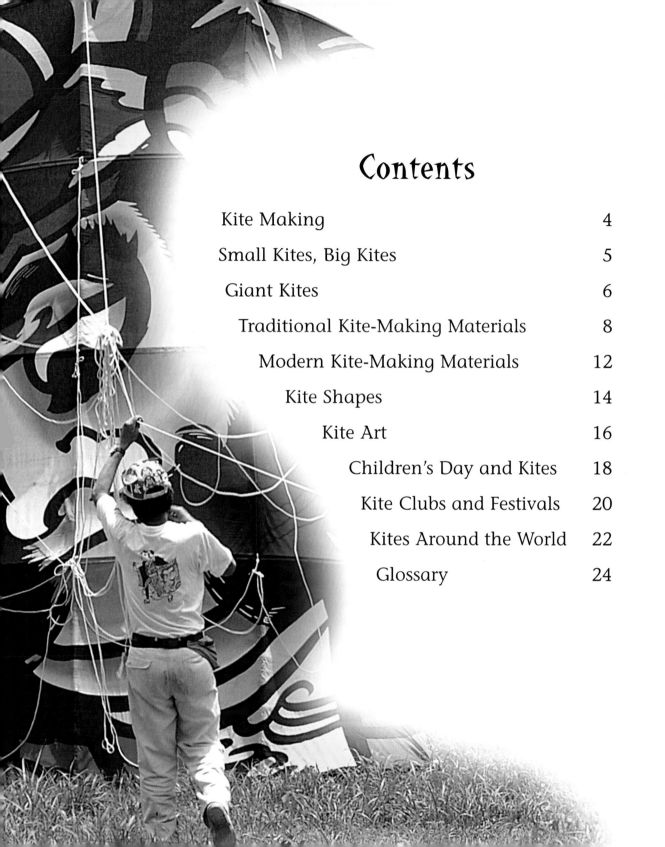

Contents

Kite Making

A kitemaster with one of his dragon kites

Kite making is an art. It requires skill and imagination. Some kitemakers have been making kites all their lives. They take pride in their kites and make sure that each one can fly.

Small Kites, Big Kites

In Japan, there are small kites, middle-sized kites, and giant kites.

The smallest kites, $1\frac{1}{2}$ to $2\frac{1}{2}$ inches high (or even smaller), are called miniatures. They may be made in the shape of insects, birds, animals, and heroes.

Most kites are up to 78 inches high. A kitemaker, working alone, can easily make these kites. You and your family members can easily fly them.

You can fly a small kite all by yourself, but not a giant one. When the wind lifts a giant kite, you too will rise up in the air!

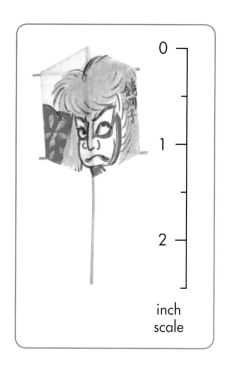

0

1

2

inch scale

A miniature kite is smaller than a pen.

Giant Kites

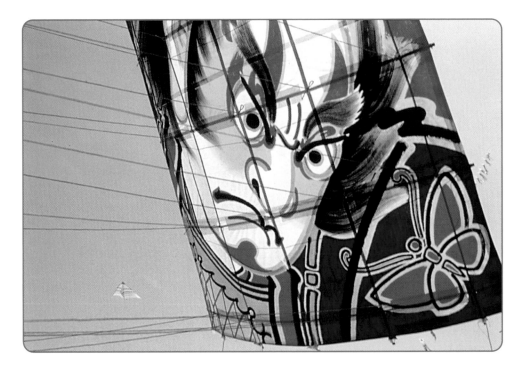

A giant *Shirone-daku* kite, from the town of Shirone in Japan

To make a giant kite, the kitemaker has a team of helpers. Giant kites can be as high as a two-story house and as heavy as a big car.

To fly such a kite, it takes from 10 to 20 adults. Some of the largest giant kites are called *odako*.

A kite-flyer preparing
to fly a giant kite

A giant kite is very heavy
because, on the underside
of the kite, there is a lot
of bamboo to keep it straight
and firm.

Traditional Kite-Making Materials

A kitemaker is preparing a kite for flying.
The bamboo spars on the back of the kite can be seen.

A long time ago in Japan, the frames and sails of kites were made from bamboo and paper. The kites would then be painted by hand.

Today, most kitemakers still like using bamboo, paper, and paint. They always use these materials to make kites for a traditional kite festival.

Bamboo

A kitemaker working with bamboo spars to make kites

A kite must have a strong framework to support it. Bamboo is used for the frame because it is strong and light. The pieces of the frame are called *spars*.

The kitemaker can bend bamboo stems because they are flexible. The bamboo can be heated and bent to make many different shapes.

Paper

A group of paper kites flying in the wind

A kite flies when the wind catches its sail. The sail is usually made of paper. The paper is made by hand from the fibers of plants, such as the mulberry tree. This paper is called *washi*. To make a strong sail, kitemakers need strong *washi*.

Paint

A kitemaker painting his kite

Most kitemakers paint the designs on kites with watercolor paint. Usually, the designs are bright and bold, made with thick and thin brushstrokes.

Sometimes the kitemakers draw outlines in wax or ink first. This stops the watercolor paint from running, or spreading over the paper.

Modern Kite-Making Materials

A modern kite uses modern materials like fiberglass.

Some kitemakers use modern materials to make kites. They use fiberglass for the spars. For the sails, they use nylon, plastic, or vinyl sheeting.

Nylon, plastic and vinyl last longer than paper does because they are more weatherproof.

Some kitemakers mix traditional and modern materials.

Preparing to fly a giant kite made of traditional and modern materials.
The spars are made of bamboo and the sails are made of vinyl sheeting.

Kite Shapes

People in different parts of Japan make different kite shapes and designs. This is because some areas of Japan have very strong winds, so they need a stronger kite. Also, in some parts of Japan, there is not enough bamboo for kite making, so other materials are used for making spars.

KITE		PLACE
①	oniyosu	Mishima
②	Baramon	Goto Island
③	hata	Nagasaki
④	mattaku	Okinawa
⑤	tosa	Kochi
⑥	Yokaichi-odako	Yokaichi
⑦	abu-dako	Nagoya

④

OKINAWA

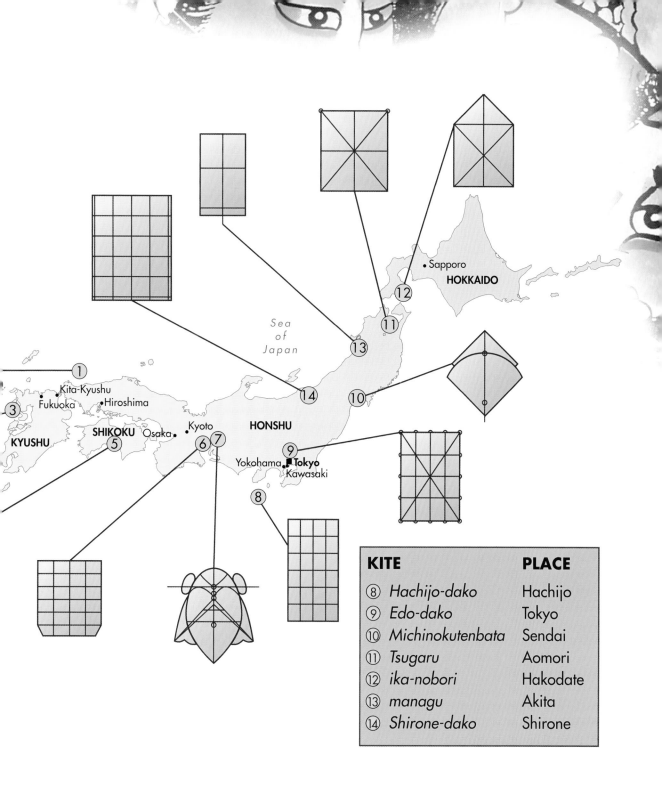

KITE	PLACE
⑧ *Hachijo-dako*	Hachijo
⑨ *Edo-dako*	Tokyo
⑩ *Michinokutenbata*	Sendai
⑪ *Tsugaru*	Aomori
⑫ *ika-nobori*	Hakodate
⑬ *managu*	Akita
⑭ *Shirone-dako*	Shirone

Kite Art

Some kites are made in the shapes of birds, such as an eagle or a hawk.

The bright colors and strong designs of kites can be seen even when flying high.

Japanese kites are often colorfully painted and beautifully designed. Pictures on Japanese kites show Japanese legends, kabuki theatre, heroes, and ancient gods.

Japanese gods, such as the Seven Gods of Happiness,
are painted on kites.

Children's Day and Kites

This kite shows Kintaro the Golden Boy.

On May 5, which is Children's Day in Japan, kite flying is a special activity. Kintaro, the hero of young boys, can be seen on many kites. He is often shown wrestling with beasts or goblins, or riding a giant carp.

This kite shows Momotaro the Peach Boy.

In Japan, everyone loves flying kites. The favorite kite of Japanese children is the "Momotaro," named after the hero of a folk tale, Momotaro the Peach Boy.

Kite Clubs and Festivals

Children making kites
at a workshop

Children holding their
completed kites

There are many kite clubs in Japan. Kitemakers teach people how to make kites at workshops.

A kite festival in Japan

Kite festivals are very popular. Since the winter is very cold, kites are mostly flown in the spring and summer months. Many tourists visit Japan in the summer to watch the kite flying.

Kites Around the World

A kite festival in Centennial Park, Sydney, Australia

   Countries such as the United States, Australia, and France now have their own kite festivals.

A kite festival in Dieppe, France

A kite festival in Washington State, USA

Glossary

fiberglass	a special, very light material partly made of glass
fibers	fine threads of a material
flexible	easily bent
folk tale	a story from a long time ago, usually about make-believe creatures and people
framework	parts fitted together to give support to something
imagination	the power of having new ideas
kabuki	traditional Japanese drama with singing, dancing, and acting, by men only
miniature	a tiny object that looks exactly like a larger one
outline	shape
sheeting	large and flat piece of material
skill	experience
spar	pole used to support a structure
traditional	related to very old customs and ways of doing or making something
weatherproof	protected from the weather
workshop	a special meeting to discuss ideas and ways of doing or making something